SPOTLIGH

THE FIRST WORLD WAR

Michael Gibson

Wayland

SPOTLIGHT ON HISTORY

Spotlight on the Age of Exploration and Discovery
Spotlight on the Age of Revolution
Spotlight on Elizabethan England
Spotlight on the First World War
Spotlight on the Industrial Revolution
Spotlight on Post-War Europe
Spotlight on the Second World War
Spotlight on the Victorians

Cover illustration: Over the top by John Nash

First published in 1985 by
Wayland (Publishers) Ltd
49 Lansdowne Place, Hove
East Sussex BN3 1HF, England

ISBN 0 85078 565 0

Typeset, printed and bound in the UK by
The Pitman Press, Bath

CONTENTS

1 THE BALANCE OF POWER

Modern European history has been dominated by the fear that one nation will become all-powerful. This very nearly happened at the beginning of the nineteenth century, when the French Emperor, Napoleon, threatened to conquer Europe. To prevent this, a coalition including Britain, Russia and Austria was created. Eventually, Napoleon was defeated and a balance of power established.

The German army on a military exercise in the 1880s. By 1914, Germany had the best-trained and best-equipped army in Europe.

HMS Dreadnought, *launched in 1906. This British warship was much more powerful than others of the period. Soon Germany and the United States also began to build ships of the Dreadnought class.*

The age of revolution

Thereafter, throughout the nineteenth century, the European powers—Britain, France, Russia, Prussia and Austria—strove to maintain this balance. They believed that war could be prevented as long as no one nation became too powerful and ambitious. They were also drawn together by fear of revolution. In every European country, the middle and lower classes were dissatisfied with their living conditions and lack of political power. The kings and emperors who ruled Europe were determined at all costs to prevent major social changes. But a series of revolutions in 1830 and 1848 forced them to allow more power to the middle classes and this usually led to the granting of some kind of constitution. Nevertheless, in spite of many concessions, the kings and emperors, advised by their ministers, remained in control of policy-making, except in the case of Britain which was ruled by a government responsible to Parliament and of France which was a republic for most of the period.

Tsar Nicholas II of Russia inspecting the mechanism of a gun during a review of the French army.

While the European rulers were desperately trying to hold on to their power, an industrial revolution was taking place. The invention of the steam engine gradually led to the development of the factory system and the growth of large towns. Goods could now be manufactured cheaply and swiftly. The main manufacturing nations, particularly Britain, France and the new German Empire, which came into being in 1871, needed new markets and sources of raw materials. As a result, these nations, known as the Great Powers, took part in the so-called 'Grab' for Africa and China. The whole world became the scene for European rivalries.

The second half of the nineteenth century also saw a military revolution. Muskets and cannon were replaced by rifles and breech-loading artillery. The cavalry declined in importance as various kinds of machine gun were introduced. Screw-propelled ironclad battleships and cruisers took the place of wooden sailing vessels. The invention of railways and steamships revolutionized travel and transport as well as war. People and goods could now be moved quickly from one part of the world to another.

King George V of Britain (right) *and Tsar Nicholas II of Russia were first cousins.*

The German Kaiser, Wilhelm II, also a cousin of King George V, inspecting a guard of honour.

Crises and alliances

Throughout the nineteenth century, the fact that the Great Powers were afraid of each other prevented the outbreak of a major war, although many 'little' wars were fought. However, as their economic and colonial rivalry created serious friction, the Great Powers sought a means of binding their friends even more closely to them. The alliance system was the result. During the second half of the nineteenth and the beginning of the twentieth century, the Triple Alliance of Germany, Austria and Italy and the Triple Entente of France, Russia and Britain were formed. Most of the treaties upon which these alliances were based involved promises of military help when a member state was attacked. Only Britain made no official military commitment, although her senior military advisors consulted with those of France and Russia and made their plans for war in the light of these discussions.

By the beginning of the twentieth century, Europe and indeed the world, was divided into 'two armed camps', and any disagreement between the rival groups could have led to war. In fact there were a series of confrontations, including the Algeciras (1905) and Agadir (1911) Incidents. However, on these occasions, the Great Powers managed to reach an agreement without fighting.

The origins of war

Why did the First World War break out? Its causes were deep-seated and complex. Some historians put forward the theory of repressed nationalism as the main cause: the empires of Russia, Austria and Turkey contained numerous peoples with different cultures, languages and hopes and many of these peoples wanted to be independent. The Great Powers feared that their empires would collapse if they gave them self-government.

In their struggle to build up overseas colonial empires, the Great Powers continually clashed. Each feared their rivals and sought to overtake them in the search for overseas markets and cheap sources of raw materials. Marxist and many other historians believe that this economic imperialism was the major cause of the war.

All the Great Powers felt threatened in one way or another. Each had serious grievances. France wanted to regain the provinces of Alsace and Lorraine, lost to Germany after the Franco-Prussian War in 1870. Russia wanted to obtain control of the Bosphorus and the Dardenelles so that she could have open access to the Mediterranean Sea. Italy dreamed of obtaining the Italian-speaking lands under Austrian control, *Italia irredenta*. Austria needed to take over more lands in the Balkans to prop up her tottering empire. The Turkish empire too, was crumbling and its peoples needed some cause to divert their attention away from their grievances; they were particularly

The funeral of King Edward VII of Great Britain in 1910, the last time that the future rivals of the Great War met peaceably, to mourn the death of a relative.

anxious to regain Cyprus and Egypt. Britain feared for the safety of her trade routes across the Mediterranean, and through the Suez Canal and the Red Sea to India; moreover, her once undisputed supremacy was being challenged by Imperial Germany. Germany was disappointed with the lands she had obtained in Africa and China and felt that she needed to expand further.

Militarism greatly increased the possibility of war. The rival groups of powers vied with each other in building up larger and larger armies and navies. Each believed that military strength would deter aggressive action on the part of its rivals. Unfortunately, this state of affairs gave too much power to the generals and admirals, many of whom felt they could only prove themselves in war. Often the politicians failed to control their military and naval leaders.

As the historian, A. J. P. Taylor, wrote, 'Nowhere was there conscious determination to provoke war. Statesmen miscalculated. They used the instruments of bluff and threat which had proved effective on previous occasions. This time things went wrong.'

2 ARMAGEDDON

The Balkans, in south-east Europe, had long been in dispute between the Great Powers. Originally, these territories had formed part of the Turkish Empire. The Russians regarded themselves as the natural protector of the Balkans, as most of the inhabitants were Orthodox Christians like themselves. The Austrians also wanted to extend their influence over an area next to their empire. In addition, there were a number of vigorous independent states, including Serbia, Greece, Romania and Bulgaria, who hoped to extend their territory.

Archduke Franz Ferdinand of Austria and his wife leaving the town hall in Sarajevo, a few minutes before their assassination on 28th June 1914.

Sarajevo

In 1908, the Austrians annexed the important provinces of Bosnia and Herzegovina, to the anger of the Russians. In 1912, the independent Balkan states set about driving the Turks out of their remaining territory in Europe. As soon as they succeeded, they quarrelled among themselves and the Great Powers had to intervene to bring the second Balkan War (1913) to an end.

The Balkans were a seething cauldron of discontent. The Slavs, one of its most numerous peoples, were determined to free all the members of their race. They created a number of secret societies, including one called the Black Hand. Members of this group decided to assassinate Archduke Franz Ferdinand of Austria during a state

The assassin Gavrilo Princip is arrested. Austria suspected Serbian involvement in the plot to kill the Archduke, and after delivering an ultimatum, declared war on Serbia on 23rd July 1914.

visit to Sarajevo, the capital of Bosnia. On 28th June 1914, the car carrying the Archduke and his wife took a wrong turning. As it reversed, Gavrilo Princip shot and fatally wounded Franz Ferdinand and his wife.

None of the European governments thought this outrage was of major importance. Austria demanded that Serbia take a number of steps to suppress the Black Hand. The Serbians resentfully agreed to most but not all of these demands. The Austrian High Command, led by General Conrad von Hotzendorff, insisted that the army be allowed to make an example of Serbia, not thinking that such an unimportant affair would lead to world war. Wilhelm II, the Emperor of Germany, commented foolishly; 'The Serbs must be disposed of and soon.'

War

On 25th July, Austria delivered an ultimatum to Serbia and, when she failed to comply with its demands, declared war. When Russia protested, General Helmuth von Moltke, the Chief of the German

Belgian refugees arrive in Britain, fleeing from the German army which invaded their country on 4th August 1914.

General Staff, wrote to General Conrad, his Austrian opposite number: 'Stand firm against Russian mobilization. Austria-Hungary must be preserved, mobilize at once against Russia. Germany will mobilize.' Wilhelm II told his Chancellor, Bethmann-Hollweg: 'even if war should occur between Austria-Hungary and Russia, [Austria] might be assured that Germany would side with her.'

In the circumstances, the Tsar ordered the Russian army to mobilize. This panicked the Germans. 'Russia will overwhelm us if she is not forestalled', warned the German Foreign Minister. Faced by the threat of a full-blooded Russian attack, the Germans declared war. France supported her ally Russia while Britain wavered. King George V of Britain noted in his diary:

> 'August 1. Saw Sir Edward Grey (the British Foreign Secretary), Germany declared war on Russia at 7.30 this evening & the

A battalion of Britain's 'New Army' on its way to defend Belgium against the invading Germans.

German Ambassador left Petersburg. Whether we shall be dragged in too God only knows, but we shall not send Expeditionary Force of the Army now. France is begging us to come to their assistance. At this moment public opinion here is dead against our joining in the War but I think it will be impossible to keep out of it as we cannot allow France to be smashed . . .

August 3. . . . Public opinion since Grey made his statement in House [of Commons] today, that we should not allow Germany to pass through English Channel & that we should not allow her troops to pass through Belgium, has entirely changed, & now everyone is for war & helping our friends. Orders for mobilization of the army will be issued at once.

August 4. . . . I held a Council at 10.45 to declare War with Germany; it is a terrible catastrophe but it is not our fault . . .'

French and British troops pass each other on a road near the battle front.

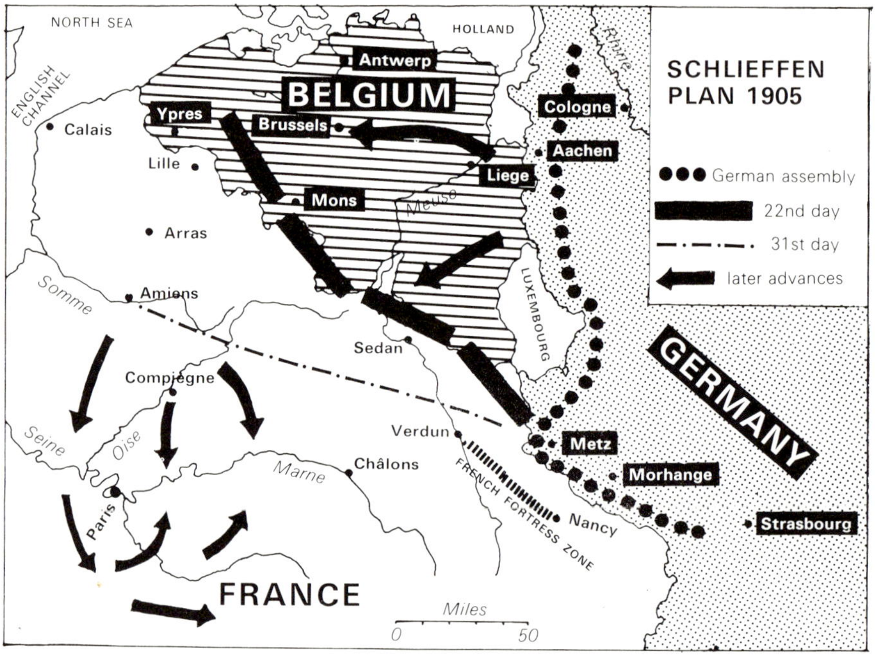

By early August, the Central Powers (Germany and Austria) were at war with the Entente Powers or Allies (Russia, France and Britain). Twenty-two other countries including Turkey, Italy, Portugal, Greece, Bulgaria, Romania, the USA, Japan and China joined in later. 'In 1914', wrote A. J. P. Taylor, 'each of the great powers lacked a statesman who could see beyond the immediacy of events and pull his country back from the abyss.'

The Schlieffen Plan

The Germans, who had always dreaded having to fight on both their western and eastern frontiers at the same time, had developed a plan drawn up in 1905, the Schlieffen Plan, which would enable them to win the war with one great blow. They intended to trick the French into believing that their main attack was to be made through Lorraine, while they concentrated their forces for an assault on Paris through Belgium. In the meantime, German forces in the east were to fight a delaying action against the Russians.

At first all went well. The French rushed the pick of their army to meet the attack in Lorraine and suffered heavy casualties. The Germans swept through Belgium into northern France, driving the British Expeditionary Force, 'that contemptible little army', as Wilhelm II called it, before them. However, the Allies fought harder than expected and slowed down the German advance so that the

British and German soldiers meet in No-Man's Land, between the battle lines in France, to celebrate the first Christmas of the war.

French were able to send reinforcements by train to the threatened areas.

On 30th August the Germans passed to the east of Paris instead of encircling it. To their surprise, the Allies counterattacked and won the Battle of the Marne. 'At the moment when the battle on which the fate of the country depended was about to open', General Joffre, the French Commander-in-Chief, recorded, 'the German High Command, from its headquarters in distant Luxembourg, knew almost nothing of what was happening on the battlefield.' The Schlieffen Plan had failed. The Germans took up a position behind the River Aisne and dug in. By the end of 1914, a complex series of trenches stretched from the shores of the North Sea to Switzerland. Hundreds of thousands of young men were to give their lives in an effort to breach these defences.

In the middle of all the horror of war, there was one small gleam of humanity. On Christmas Day 1914, fighting stopped all along the Western Front and soldiers of both sides made friends, swopped cigarettes and played football. This was to be the only pause in four-and-a-half years of slaughter.

3 THE WESTERN FRONT

After the failure of the Schlieffen Plan in 1914, the Chief of the German General Staff, von Moltke, was replaced by General von Falkenhayn. In 1915, Falkenhayn decided to fight defensively in the west while making an all-out effort to knock the Russians out of the war. As a result, the Allies took the initiative on the Western Front and launched offensives in Artois and Champagne. In spite of 190,000 French, 50,000 British and 140,000 German casualties, little progress was made by either side. Meanwhile, the German offensive in the east failed to destroy the Russian army.

British troops bringing guns and equipment up to the front line.

French troops marching to the defence of Verdun, in 1916.

The deadlock

In 1916, Falkenhayn planned to 'lure France into a great battle at Verdun and allow her to destroy herself'. As the city of Verdun was associated with France's most glorious victories (in 1792 and again in 1870), Falkenhayn calculated that the French would sacrifice anything to prevent its loss. 'The essential question,' he wrote, 'is not to take Verdun . . . but to pin down the French . . . [and] bleed them white.' The battle lasted nearly ten months and 420,000 men were killed and another 800,000 wounded. A French officer described the effect of the German bombardment: 'We came along the Haumont sap, under flanking shell-fire. The trench filled up with corpses all along—men were dying there in the mud, some already with a death rattle, others begging for water, others still screaming for us to end their agony.' Of all the battles of the First World War, Verdun was probably the worst.

British and Commonwealth troops outside their dug-outs; during the battle of the Somme, 1916.

The other great battle on the Western Front in 1916 took place along the River Somme. The French were in great difficulties and their Chief of Staff, General Joffre, informed General Haig, the British Commander-in-Chief, that, 'Unless the British attack along the Somme, the French Army will cease to exist.' The Allies attacked with great courage but lost 500,000 men killed, wounded or taken prisoner.

Trench warfare

Trench warfare was a living hell for the soldiers on both sides. A German officer vividly described a typical British attack:

> 'The intense bombardment was realized by all to be the prelude to an infantry assault sooner or later. The men in the dug-outs therefore waited ready, belts full of hand grenades . . . At 7.30 a.m. the hurricane of shells ceased . . . The machine guns were pulled out of the dugouts and hurriedly placed in position . . . a series of extended lines of infantry were seen moving forward

Soldiers rest or write a last letter home before leaving the shelter of the trench to attack the enemy lines.

> from the British trenches . . . A few minutes later, when the leading British line was within a hundred yards, the rattle of machine gun and rifle broke out along the whole line . . . Whole sections seemed to fall . . . The advance rapidly crumpled under this hail of shells and bullets.'

It is difficult to imagine what the soldiers felt like waiting to 'go over the top'. A French officer recalled:

> 'The hours went by slowly and inexorably; we could not even swallow for tension; there was always the thought—in a few hours where shall I be, here, or one of these vile corpses, torn to bits by shell. The moment comes . . . I shouted, "Forward", and then a red explosion blinded me and threw me to the ground . . .'

To the horrors of shelling and machine gun fire, mustard gas was soon added. 'It burned my throat', wrote a Frenchman, 'caused pains in my chest and made breathing all but impossible. I spat blood and suffered dizziness'. Many victims suffered severe eye injuries and some were blinded.

British infantry going 'over the top' to attack the enemy.

A drawing of the French army's heroic defence of Verdun.

A gas attack caused panic, as the poet Wilfred Owen, a British officer, described:

> 'Gas! Gas! Quick boys!—An ecstasy of fumbling
> Fitting the clumsy helmets just in time;
> But someone still was yelling out and stumbling
> And floundering like a man in fire or lime.'

For many men it seemed that the deadlock would never end and bombardments followed by attacks would go on for ever more. A few men went mad, some deserted and were shot and many had mental breakdowns due to shell shock.

British stretcher-bearers sinking in the mud as they carry away a wounded soldier at the battle of Passchendaele, 1917.

From Passchendaele to the Armistice

At the end of 1916, Falkenhayn was replaced as Chief of the German General Staff by Paul von Hindenburg. The new commander immediately ordered the preparation of a new system of trenches—the Hindenburg Line—to be dug behind the existing system. Early in 1917, the Germans fell back on this superb structure with its concrete machine gun emplacements and network of light railways to carry men and materials to and from the Front. The Allied commanders, the 'donkeys', as their men called them, had learnt nothing from previous attacks and continued to hurl their troops at the new defensive wall.

Allied losses were so great that the exhausted French Army started to break up and the British had to take over a larger sector of the Front. Between 11th July and 6th November, the dreadful battle of Passchendaele took place during one of the wettest summers on record. According to the British Official History, 'The shelled areas

A German machine-gun post which has been destroyed by Allied troops.

near the Front became a barrier of swamp . . . passable only by a few well-defined tracks which became targets for the enemy's artillery; and to leave the tracks was to risk death by drowning.'

Casualties were appalling and yet there seemed to be no hope of a breakthrough. However, there were two gleams of hope amidst all the pessimism. One was the success of a new invention, the tank. At the Battle of Cambrai on 20th November 1917, a German correspondent wrote: 'The monsters approached slowly . . . Nothing impeded them . . . Someone in the trenches said, "The devil is coming" . . . Tongues of flame leapt from the sides of the iron caterpillars . . . the English infantry came in waves behind.' 10,000 Germans and 200 guns were captured. Unfortunately, the British did not make the most of their advantage and the Germans were quick to produce tanks of their own. The second source of hope was the arrival of American troops in France, where they helped to raise the Allies' sagging morale. The

Kaiser Wilhelm II inspects a detachment of his troops.

United States declared war on Germany on 6th April 1917, following the loss of American ships, sunk by German U-boats.

By the beginning of 1918, Hindenburg and his Chief of Staff, General Ludendorff, were convinced that time was running out. Hindenburg told Wilhelm II: 'In order to secure the political and economic situation in the world we need, we must defeat the Western Powers.' In March, a huge German offensive pushed back the Allies, causing their politicians to panic. Lord Milner, the British Minister for War, told Prime Minister Lloyd George: 'We must be prepared for France and Italy both being beaten to their knees. In that case the German-Austro-Turk-Bulgar bloc will master all Europe and Northern and Central Asia.'

However, in this extreme emergency, the Allies forgot their rivalries and appointed Marshal Ferdinand Foch Commander-in-Chief of the

Allied Armies in France. He counterattacked when the Germans least expected it and forced them back. Ludendorff wrote of this as the 'Black Day': 'August 8 marked the decline of our military power and took from me the hope . . . of discovering some strategic expedient that would restore the situation in our favour.' On 4th October 1918, the Germans requested an armistice.

Fighting continued during the negotiations and the German armies were pushed out of northern France and Belgium. On 11th November, the troops on the Western Front learned that an armistice had been signed: 'A few cheers were raised', a soldier recalled, 'but otherwise they [the troops] received this great event with calm.'

The arrival of the first American troops in France, in July 1918.

4 THE EASTERN FRONT

When the Germans invaded northern France in 1914, the Allies relied on the 'Russian Steamroller' to give them relief and draw off German reinforcements. In August, Grand Duke Nicholas, the Russian Commander-in-Chief, ordered his armies into East Prussia.

Russian defeat

For a time all went well and the Russian armies made good progress. Then, the Germans placed Paul von Hindenburg and Erich von Ludendorff in charge of their Eastern armies. These two generals formed the most effective military partnership of the war. Within a few days, the Russians had been badly defeated at the battles of Tannenberg and the Masurian Lakes, in East Prussia. 'Whole army corps [of Russians] advanced,' wrote a German newspaper reporter, 'without bread or oats and had to have recourse to their reserve rations . . . discipline was bad . . . . nerves were so shaken that the troops fired at

Russian troops at a review in 1914.

Russian troops manoeuvring heavy guns in snow on the Eastern Front.

anyone.' On 31st August, Hindenburg proudly informed Wilhelm II, 'The ring around the larger part of the Russian army was closed yesterday . . . We have already taken more than 60,000 prisoners . . . The booty is immense.' However, the Russian armies were doing well elsewhere: they drove the Austrians out of Galicia (part of Poland) and forced the Turks to retreat behind the Caucasus Mountains.

In 1915, Falkenhayn, the new Chief of the German General Staff, ordered Hindenburg to knock the Russians out of the war. However, before he could attempt to carry out these orders, Hindenburg had to send help to the Austrians. Large numbers of German troops were diverted to the Galician front. A combined Austro-German attack broke through the Russian lines at Gorlice in May. The Russians, who were so short of supplies that many lacked rifles, were driven out of Galicia and forced to abandon Poland.

The Russian General Deniken described the retreat from Poland:

> 'For over twelve days, the Germans swept our lines, and we could not reply, as there was nothing left . . . exhausted regiments had only bayonets to fight with . . . losses were high, the ranks got thinner and thinner. Two regiments were destroyed almost entirely by artillery.'

Hindenburg had won a great but, as it turned out, indecisive victory.

German infantry await a Russian attack along the banks of the River Vistula, in Poland.

In 1917, Lenin, the Russian revolutionary leader, was helped by the Germans to return from exile to Russia.

The Brusilov attack

The Germans offered the Russians a compromise peace, but Tsar Nicholas II refused to desert his allies. Instead, he made himself Commander-in-Chief of his armies. In 1916, he called for a great effort against the Austrians. General Brusilov fought a brilliant campaign and regained Galicia, capturing 400,000 prisoners and 500 guns. This magnificent effort may well have saved Britain, France and Italy from defeat in 1916 as the Germans were forced to remove troops from the Western Front to bolster up their allies. However, Russia was exhausted.

The Russians had suffered a million casualties. Their government was in chaos, their communications network was breaking down, prices were rising at a fantastic rate and food and fuel were in short supply. The winter of 1916–17 was bitter even by Russian standards and her people could stand no more. In March 1917, the Tsar was forced to abdicate and the Germans helped Lenin, the Bolshevik revolutionary leader, to return to Russia. A provisional government was set up which decided to honour the promises made by the previous government to her allies and in July the Russian armies launched another great assault on the Germans. The result of the assault was the total defeat and break-up of the Russian armies. Ordinary soldiers murdered their officers and fled from the battlefield. General Kornilov tried to seize control of the government, but was defeated. In November 1917, the Bolsheviks rose and seized Petrograd, Moscow and other leading Russian towns. In a remarkably short time, Lenin was in virtual control of Russia.

A scene in Petrograd (modern Leningrad) during the Bolshevik Revolution of 1917.

Brest-Litovsk

The Bolsheviks demanded a peace that would be 'fair for all nationalities without exception,' but the Germans scented total victory and were unimpressed. German armies plunged deep into Russia, seizing the Baltic Provinces and the Ukraine. Although most Bolsheviks wanted to attack the invaders, Lenin refused to allow this. 'Give me an army of 100,000 men which will not tremble before the enemy', he challenged his critics. When this was not forthcoming, he insisted that peace was essential if the revolution was to succeed. The Bolsheviks made peace with the Germans at Brest-Litovsk in March 1918. The treaty seemed a terrible disaster to most Russians as it stripped them of a quarter of their population, their best agricultural land, three-quarters of their iron and coal supplies and half of their industrial plant. However, Lenin was right. The ending of the war ensured the success of the Bolshevik Revolution.

The withdrawal of Russia from the war was a tremendous blow to the Allies. As Hindenburg commented, 'No longer threatened in the rear, we [the Germans] can turn to the great decision in the West and must now address ourselves to this passage of arms.' Although the Germans had to maintain a strong military presence in the conquered lands, many regiments were transferred to the Western Front, where they played an important part in the last great struggle. Moreover, Lenin struck another blow at the Allies by publishing their secret treaties, in which they had promised each other all kinds of advantages should they win the war. The exposure of these treaties did little to enhance the reputation of the Allies with the neutral peoples of the world.

5 THE ITALIAN FRONT

When the first World War broke out, Italy did not join the Central Powers in spite of her membership of the Triple Alliance. However, the Italian government was very anxious to acquire the territories of the Austrian Tyrol, Istria and Trieste, which had a total population of 750,000 Italians. Austria, however, refused to cede these lands. The Allies, who were desperate for help in their struggle with the Central Powers, promised these areas to Italy if she would

A British regiment marching to join Italian troops at the River Piave in Austria-Hungary, near the border with Italy.

Italian troops in a mountain pass near the River Piave, in 1918.

enter the war on their side. Italy was unable to resist this bribe and declared war on Austria on 23rd May 1915.

Italian offensive

The Italians were not a major military power. They had fared badly in a war with the Turks in Libya only three years earlier. Nevertheless, they launched an offensive along the River Isonzo in Austria-Hungary. But as the Italian writer, Piero Pieri, noted, 'The river could not be crossed until the mountains had been seized, and the mountains could not be seized until the river had been crossed.' There were to be eleven battles along the banks of this river between 1915 and 1917. On each occasion, it was the Italians who attacked because the Austrians had their hands full trying to keep the Russians and Serbs at bay.

The Italians obtained little territory and suffered heavy casualties in return. Falkenhayn, the Chief of the German General Staff, commented gleefully, 'The hopes placed in the defensive strength of the mountainous territory of the Austro-Hungarian and Italian frontier were altogether fulfilled.' In spite of what amounted to a defeat, General Cadorna, the Italian Commander-in-Chief, persisted with his offensive approach for three years.

Mountain warfare

The style of warfare that took place along the Italian front contrasted vividly with that of the Western trenches. Many battles, like the following one described by an Italian war correspondent, were fought in the snow:

> 'On the evening of April 11th three detachments of skiatori [skiers], dressed in white and equipped with white covered muskets and machine guns started for the Brizio Pass. Overtaken by a terrible tormenta [storm], they lost their way and wandered about during the night unaware of the location of one another, for no signalling or whistling was allowed. A passing moment of light at daybreak enabled them to meet and re-form. Shortly afterwards the storm ceased, the sun shone brightly and they saw the Austrians entrenched on a string of snowy slopes. Lining up in four columns spread in the shape of a fan toward the enemy, they made a quick dash, fired a volley, and sprinted forward. This manoeuvre they repeated again and again, so quickly that, despite the machine gun fire directed against them, they succeeded in reaching and completely disorganizing the enemy. The Austrians surrendered and the battle resulted in the occupation of all the heights on the edge of the glacier, the capture of fifty prisoners, two machine guns, one hundred rifles and a large amount of ammunition and supplies.'

Emperor Franz Josef of Austria-Hungary ruled over an empire of many nations. At the end of the war, this empire had dwindled to one small, German-speaking nation.

Although the Italians found it difficult to hold their own against the Austrians, they were asked to give military help to the hard-pressed Serbs, who had been badly defeated by the Bulgarians. Meanwhile, little progress was made along the Isonzo front throughout 1916 and 1917. However, as the Austrian troops were becoming demoralized by being perpetually on the defensive, General Conrad, their Commander-in-Chief, decided to attack the Italians in 1917.

Caporetto and Vittorio Veneto

On 24th October 1917, the Austro-German forces started a vast bombardment of high explosive and gas shells. The gas proved to be particularly effective as the Italian soldiers' gas masks were defective. The Italian front line crumpled and many of the troops deserted. This was hardly surprising as few of them felt they had anything to fight for. In the circumstances, Italian morale collapsed and their armies retreated, first behind the Tagliamento and then behind the Piave rivers. In the defeat at Caporetto, 10,000 Italians were killed, 30,000 wounded and 230,000 captured.

Strangely, this disaster strengthened Italian resolve. Artillery and munitions were manufactured in vast quantities. General Cadorna was replaced by General Diaz. The Italian armies held the line along the River Piave. Throughout the first half of 1918, the struggle continued without any real progress being made by either side. Foch, the Allied Commander-in-Chief in France, asked Diaz to attack the exhausted Austrian army so that the Germans would have to send help or allow them to surrender. Diaz refused, arguing that his armies were not strong enough to go on to the offensive.

In the meantime, Hindenburg, the Chief of the German General Staff, asked his Austrian allies to make a special effort against the Italians. Gallantly, if foolishly, Austrian forces attacked all along the Trentino and Piave fronts on 15th June 1918. They were bloodily repulsed. But still Diaz refused to order his men to advance. At last the exhausted Austrians asked for an armistice. Seizing the opportunity, the Italians advanced, sweeping all before them. The Austrian army was in a state of collapse. Many regiments mutinied and marched off to their homelands. For Italy, the war ended with the brilliant victory of Vittorio Veneto. No less than 500,000 Austrian troops were captured. On 3rd November, an armistice was signed.

In spite of this final triumph, the war had been a disaster for Italy. She had allowed herself to be lured into it by the promise of lands to which the Allies had no claim. The expense of the war ruined her economy. In addition, she had suffered 650,000 casualties. The only hope for Italian democracy was that the Allies would honour the promises they made in 1915 and hand over the Italian-speaking territories under Austrian control—*Italia irredenta*. This hope was to be largely disappointed.

Italian civilians being supplied with food by the Red Cross.

6 THE WAR AGAINST THE TURKS

The Turks allied themselves with the Central Powers in October 1914, because they hated and feared the Russians, with whom they had been fighting almost continuously for hundreds of years. They were also determined to regain Cyprus and Egypt which they had lost to Britain. The war started badly for them when they were defeated by the Russians and forced to withdraw behind the Caucasus Mountains.

Sultan Muhammed V of Turkey, greeting the Kaiser in 1917.

Winston Churchill, First Lord of the Admiralty (right) *consults with Admiral of the Fleet Lord Fisher, before the disastrous Gallipoli landings.*

The Dardanelles

In Britain, a group of politicians, led by Lloyd George and Winston Churchill, believed that the war could be won by eliminating Germany's allies. If the Turks could be decisively defeated, they argued, the Germans would be forced to fight on three, instead of two, fronts. Accordingly, in 1915, the British sent a naval expedition to force a passage through the Dardanelles, a narrow strait of water connecting the Mediterranean to the Sea of Marmara and Istanbul, the capital of Turkey.

The attempt was a disaster. The British fleet found it impossible to find a way through the Turkish mines and the heavy shell fire of the shore batteries. In the weeks that followed, the Turks worked hard to improve their defences throughout the Gallipoli peninsula, which overlooked the approach to the Dardanelles. Undeterred, Churchill decided that the Dardanelles should be seized by a military force to be landed on Gallipoli. The first landings of British and Commonwealth troops took place on 25th April. 'The preparations of the enemy were excellent,' observed Liman von Sanders, the commander of the Turkish Fifth Army, 'their only defect being that they were based on reconnaissances that were too old and that they underestimated the powers of resistance of the Turkish soldier.' Many men were mown down by Turkish fire as they tried to land. Those who succeeded found themselves pinned down on the inhospitable slopes of the peninsula.

Horses being landed at Suvla Bay, on the Gallipoli peninsula.

One group landed unobserved but failed to march inland. 'It is as certain as anything can be in war,' observes the Official British History, 'that a bold advance from Y beach on the morning of 25 April must have . . . ensured a decisive victory.'

As it was, the British and Commonwealth troops had to hack out shallow trenches in the thin soils of the hillsides. Conditions were appalling. There was no shade from the burning sun during the day or protection from the cold at night. Rations were poor and many men suffered from dysentery. On 6th August, further landings took place at

Suvla Bay. But once again the Allies lost their advantage. 20,000 men sat around waiting for orders. By the time they came, Turkish guns had covered their positions. Throughout 1915, men continued to die at an alarming rate. Finally, the whole force had to be evacuated.

While the men were sweating and dying on Gallipoli, the Allies opened up another front in the Balkans, where the Serbs were in great difficulties because Bulgaria had joined the Central Powers. In October 1915, the Allies made a landing at Salonika and advanced inland. However, on being defeated by the Bulgarians, they fell back to Salonika where they remained for the rest of the war. British comedians used to joke, 'if you want a holiday, go to Salonika.' Rather late in the day, the garrison broke out and defeated the Bulgarians in September 1918.

Australian and New Zealand troops attacking at Anzac Cove, on the Gallipoli peninsula.

The Middle East

The allies were also fighting the Turks in the Middle East. The British feared that the Turks would attack Egypt and seize control of the Suez Canal. In consequence, the British invaded the Sinai Desert in 1916 and persuaded Hussein, the Sherif of Mecca, to rebel against the Turks. The Turks defeated the Arabs but committed such terrible

Russian, Italian and French troops drawing water from a well, in Salonika, in 1916.

atrocities that Arab resistance was enormously strengthened. Late in 1916, Captain T. E. Lawrence was sent to liaise with the Arab forces. He quickly won their trust and admiration and organized a series of highly effective hit-and-run attacks on Turkish positions and communications.

In the following extract from *The Seven Pillars of Wisdom*, Lawrence describes one such attack:

> 'Round the bend, whistling its loudest, came the train . . . I touched off under the first driving wheel of the locomotive, and the explosion was terrific. The ground spouted blackly into my face, and I was sent spinning, to sit up with the shirt torn to my shoulder and the blood dripping from long, ragged scratches in

my left arm . . . In front of me was the scalded and smoking upper half of a man. When I peered through the dust and steam of the explosion, the whole boiler of the first engine seemed to be missing. The rest of the train was badly derailed . . . In it had been Mehmed Jemal Pasha, commanding the [Turkish] Eighth Army Corps, hurrying down to defend Jerusalem against Allenby [The British Commander] . . . There had been some four hundred men on board, and the survivors, now recovered from the shock, were under shelter and shooting hard at us . . . The Turks, seeing us so quiet, began to advance up the slope. We let them come half-way, and then poured in volleys which killed some twenty and drove the others back. The ground around the train was strewn with dead . . . We were now only about forty left, and obviously could do no good against them. So we ran in batches up the little stream bed [and made good our escape].'

Colonel T. E. Lawrence, with leaders of the Arab forces in Arabia.

War in the Middle East—refugees returning to their villages.

In June 1917, the British and Arabs made a combined attack on the Turkish forces in Palestine and broke through the Gaza line. General Allenby, the British Commander-in-Chief, entered Jerusalem on Christmas Day, 1917. Throughout 1918, the Turks were pushed steadily back, until Allenby and Lawrence's Arabs reached Damascus in October 1918.

Mesopotamia

The Allies also fought the Turks in Mesopotamia (modern-day Iraq). The British feared that Mesopotamia would be used as a jumping-off point for the invasion of India and wanted to protect their oil supplies in the Persian Gulf. A joint Anglo-Indian expeditionary force landed near Basra in November 1914. After a severe defeat at the siege of Kut in 1916, the Allies gradually made their way up the valleys of the Tigris and Euphrates to Baghdad and finally reached the shores of the Caspian Sea.

By October 1918, the Turks were exhausted and signed an armistice. Defeat brought about the fall of the Sultanate, although the Ottoman ruler remained Caliph, or religious leader, until 1923.

7 WAR AT SEA AND IN THE AIR

One of the major causes of friction between Britain and Germany before the outbreak of war had been naval rivalry. Throughout the nineteenth century, the British fleet was so powerful that it could have destroyed all the rest of the world's navies put together. However, the invention of the Dreadnought class of battleship ended Britain's undisputed supremacy of the seas. The British and German shipyards produced about equal numbers of these revolutionary vessels so that no one knew who would win mastery of the seas if war broke out.

Jutland

As soon as war was declared in 1914, the British started to rid the oceans of enemy vessels. A German naval squadron under Admiral von Spee was destroyed off the Falkland Islands in December 1914, after it had defeated a smaller British fleet off Coronel in Chile, on

HMS Iron Duke. *This was the flagship of Admiral Jellicoe, Commander of the British Grand Fleet.*

The British battleship Superb *opens fire on the German High Seas Fleet at the Battle of Jutland, 31st May 1915.*

1st November. As a result, the German High Command decided not to risk its High Seas Fleet in a full-scale battle with the Royal Navy. It was ordered to remain in the Baltic and to make periodic small-scale raids. Consequently, the British had to employ many of their ships to blockade the Baltic.

The one large-scale sea battle of the war took place off Jutland on 31st May and 1st June 1916 as a result of a mistake. The German High Seas fleet ventured out without any intention of giving battle and was surprised by a British fleet led by Admiral Jellicoe. In his memoirs, Jellicoe recalled:

> 'It appeared as if all the enemy ships . . . were receiving heavy punishment . . . At 6.45 p.m., one or two torpedoes crossed the track of the rear of our battle line . . . They were apparently fired, at long range, by enemy destroyers, which were barely visible to the ships in the rear. Shortly after 6.55 p.m., the *Iron Duke* [his flag ship] passed the wreck of a ship [the *Invincible*], subsequent information showed that she was destroyed by gunfire, which caused her magazines to explode . . . (After 7.20 p.m.) the enemy turned away and showed no disposition to fight.'

A German U-boat (submarine) in port

The battle exposed weaknesses in the design of the British warships which the shipbuilders were quick to put right. Thereafter, the German fleet remained inactive and its sailors' morale fell so low that they mutinied in 1918.

Blockade and the submarine campaign

The British used their fleet to blockade the Central Powers. In this way, they were able to stop them importing food and raw materials, and from exporting trade goods. At the same time, the Germans tried to destroy the Allied control of the sea by a submarine campaign. As Admiral von Tirpitz, the Commander of the German Navy, told an American journalist in 1914, 'England wants to starve us. We can play the same game . . . We can bottle her up and destroy every ship that endeavours to break the blockade.'

German U-boats (submarines) attacked Allied merchant and fighting ships with torpedoes. These underwater missiles contained 500 lbs (226 kg) of explosive and moved through the water at 36 m.p.h. (58 km/h). In 1914, Britain had more submarines than Germany, but thereafter the Germans concentrated all their energies in producing

Passengers on board the American liner Lusitania *watch the approach of the German torpedo, which sank her on 7th May 1915.*

The last moments of the Lusitania, *which sank with the loss of 1,198 lives. This act of war by a German U-boat was largely instrumental in bringing the United States into the war in 1918.*

U-boats in large numbers. When the U-boat campaign opened in 1915, immense numbers of Allied ships were sunk. On 7th May, the *Lusitania* was torpedoed off Ireland and 1,198 passengers, including 139 Americans, were drowned. Such was the German success that they decided to launch an unrestricted campaign in 1917, even though they realized this might force the Americans into the war on the side of the Allies. Indeed, the USA declared war on Germany on 6th April 1917. However, Admiral Holtzendorff boasted to Wilhelm II: 'I guarantee on my word as a naval officer that no American will set foot on the continent.'

By this time, however, the Allies had discovered the answer to the submarine menace—the convoy system. Merchant vessels sailed in close formation, protected by warships. The invention of ASDIC (apparatus for detecting submarines) enabled the warships to pinpoint the position of enemy submarines and blow them out of the water with depth charges. As a result the number of merchant ships sunk declined rapidly and many more U-boats were destroyed.

Air power and the Red Baron

In spite of its spectacular nature, airpower was only of minor importance during the 1914–18 war. At the beginning, artillery officers were sent up in balloons to direct the fire of the big guns. Later, the Germans carried out a few attacks on British cities with large airships called Zeppelins. These raids, however, caused more fright than damage. Aeroplanes were first used for reconnaissance purposes and only later, armed with machine guns, for fighting.

During the last two years of the war, fighter aircraft on both sides struggled for command of the skies. Planes fought what were called 'dogfights', which were often conducted in a sporting manner. Captured pilots were feasted by their captors and treated with the greatest courtesy. Manfred von Richthofen, 'the Red Baron', was the most famous of these 'aces'. Here is his account of a 'dogfight' in 1916:

> 'The Englishman attempted to get behind me while I attempted to get behind him. So it went, both of us flying like madmen in a circle . . . At about a hundred metres altitude he tried to escape toward the Front by flying zigzag . . . I followed him . . . firing steadily. The Englishman had to fall. A jam in my guns almost cost me success. About fifty metres behind our lines he plunged down with a shot through the head.'

Richthofen shot down eighty enemy planes until he met Captain Brown of the Royal Flying Corps on 21st April 1918. Captain Brown wrote:

A fighter aircraft of the Royal Flying Corps.

British and German fighter planes involved in a 'dogfight' high above the battle lines.

> 'I dived down until I was on his tail, then I fired. The bullets tore into his elevator and mutilated the rear part of the plane. Flames showed where the bullets struck . . . The pilot turned around and looked back. I saw the glint of eyes behind the big goggles, then he collapsed in the seat, as the bullets whistled by him. I ceased firing.'

The Red Baron was dead. Exciting as were his exploits, they did little to affect the outcome of the war. However, Richthofen, Brown and all the other brave pilots prepared the way for their successors during the Second World War.

8 THE HOME FRONTS

Civilians everywhere received the outbreak of war with surprising enthusiasm. In Britain, although the Socialists were pledged to non-violence, most supported the war. Even the suffragettes, after some initial heart-searching, threw themselves into war work. Moreover, the opening of hostilities led to xenophobia—hatred of foreigners. Shopkeepers with foreign-sounding names had their windows broken. In Britain, Lord Battenburg was driven from his post as First Lord of the Admiralty for no better reason than his German name and ancestry. He changed the family name to Mountbatten.

The declaration of war in 1914 was enthusiastically greeted by most German people.

Volunteers, propaganda and rations

Large numbers of men everywhere volunteered for military service. In Britain, normally the most unmilitary of countries, the government was able to rely on volunteers until 1916 when compulsory conscription was reluctantly introduced. Some men were unprepared to serve,

In the summer of 1915, Lord Kitchener, Secretary of State for War, introduced an intensive campaign to recruit volunteers to replace the huge British losses in France.

for religious and moral reasons. These 'conscientious objectors' were often treated with great harshness. Young men who did not volunteer for military service were sometimes given white feathers suggesting that they were cowards.

Both sides used propaganda to increase their peoples' hatred of the enemy. Even the most creditable newspapers published false atrocity stories. The effects of these propaganda campaigns were long-lasting and helped to create irrational hatred for the peoples of the enemy nations. From the very beginning of the war, civilians on both sides only received the news their governments wanted them to hear. Even

Thousands of young American men volunteered for service after the United States declared war in 1917.

letters written by members of the armed forces to their relatives were carefully censored.

Governments everywhere called on their people to economise. In Britain, King George V set an example by giving up smoking and the drinking of alcohol—he became extremely bad tempered as a result. The naval blockades caused food prices to rise and the poor found difficulty in buying even the necessities of life. Finally, food rationing had to be introduced and prices were fixed by government agencies. Even then the people of the warring nations suffered considerably, especially those of the Central Powers. An Austrian woman wrote in her diary: 'The doctors have discovered that, even if we got the whole of our ration, this would only be sufficient to meet one fourth of the food requirements of an adult person weighing 11 stone (70 kg.)'.

Trade, industry and the workers

The whole-hearted response of most working men to the call to arms meant an almost total end to strikes during the first year of the war. So many skilled men joined the armed forces that union rules had to be relaxed to allow relatively inexperienced and unqualified workers to take their place. With the growth of the munitions industry, large numbers of new workers were required.

In Britain, the conditions in most of these new factories were far superior to those in ordinary industry. However, trade unionists and reformers often felt that the government misused its powers. Sylvia Pankhurst, a leading suffragette, complained that 'the Munitions Act was being used to prevent workers from changing their employment in order to secure higher wages or positions of greater responsibility.' And she pointed out that in the cotton trade, the same powers were used by the employers to 'deny the workers a 5 per cent increase in wages, to aid them meeting the enhanced cost of living.' As prices rose and conditions deteriorated, the number of strikes increased; there were 672 strikes in Britain in 1915 and 1,165 in 1918. On the other hand, the British government consulted trade union leaders about matters concerning labour and members of the Labour Party were included in the coalition governments which ruled Britain after 1915.

At first, the Liberal government in Britain called for 'business as usual'. But as the war entered its second full year, more and more businesses had to be turned over to full-time war production. As a result, consumer goods became scarce and trade goods were no longer available for foreign customers. In consequence, Britain lost many of her overseas markets to the Americans and Japanese. The cost of the war was so great that Britain had to advance her allies large loans which they were never able to repay. During the last stages of the war, all the Allied countries had to borrow large sums from the Americans,

A British soldier leaves for the battle front. Enthusiasm ran high during the early years of the war, despite the terrible losses.

The U-boat campaign resulted in heavy losses of merchant shipping, with consequent food shortages in British shops.

which they were expected to repay after the end of the war. These repayments delayed the Allies' economic recovery and played an important part in creating the Great Depression of the 1930s.

Important changes in employment patterns took place in many countries as a result of the war. Until 1914, domestic service had been one of the largest industries. With the growth in job opportunities, the upper and middle classes had greater and greater difficulty getting servants and this trend continued after the war. Working people wanted to live in their own homes and have more time and money with which to enjoy themselves.

Women, anti-war feeling and the war artists

Women were one of the few groups to improve their situation during the war. Their labour was required in the metal industries, engineering, transport and agriculture as well as in the munitions works. After the war, women in Britain, America, Germany, Russia and Austria obtained the right to vote in general elections. The 'world's largest minority group' was starting on the road towards equality.

During 1917 and 1918, a minority of people in all countries expressed anti-war feelings. In Britain, a number of serving officers, including the poet Siegfried Sassoon, openly stated their misgivings.

The role of women in Britain changed dramatically during the war. They now had to take on jobs previously always done by men.

This poster was aimed at those who had doubts about joining up.

Women assembling aeroplane parts in a munitions factory.

Most people dismissed these criticisms as disloyalty or the rantings of cowards and the mentally unstable. However, disillusionment gradually spread, particularly among the Central Powers, where it helped to bring the war to an end. For instance, the German navy mutinied, and the spirit of revolution spread across the country, infecting the army. The Kaiser abdicated on 10th November and on 11th November the Armistice was signed. The people of the Austrian Empire, too, broke up into their different nationalities before the Armistice was signed. In the end, the long-suffering civilians demanded that their political masters heed their wishes.

Curiously, out of the horror of war arose paintings, novels and poems like this one by Major John McCrae:

'We are the Dead. Short days ago
We lived, felt dawn, saw sunset glow,
Loved and were loved, and now we lie
In Flanders Fields.
Take up our quarrel with the foes,
To you from failing hands we throw
The Torch; be yours to hold it high.
If ye break faith with us who die
We shall not sleep, though Poppies grow
In Flanders Fields.'

Great advances were also made in medicine, in the production of motorized vehicles and electronics. Although the war had destroyed a whole generation of young men and left a legacy of hatred and fear, it also left a spirit of hope for the future.

Wives and mothers anxiously scanning the daily casualty lists.

9 HOW THE PEACE WAS LOST

Between 1914 and 1918, 8,538,315 members of the Armed Forces were killed and 21,219,452 wounded. In addition, 12,618,000 civilians died from military action, starvation and exposure. The war is thought to have cost $375 billion. Everyone expected economic, social and political disaster to follow.

The Treaty of Versailles

The first thing the victors had to do was draw up what they considered equitable (fair) peace treaties with the vanquished. By the Treaty of Versailles, the Allies stripped Germany of Alsace-Lorraine, Upper Silesia and her entire overseas empire. Worse still, most of her merchant navy was seized by the Allies. Germany was ordered to deliver 25 million tons of coal to the Allies each year. The west bank of the Rhine was to be occupied by Allied troops. The German army was

On 19th November 1918, the Armistice was signed in Marshal Foch's railway coach headquarters, in a siding near Compiégne, in France.

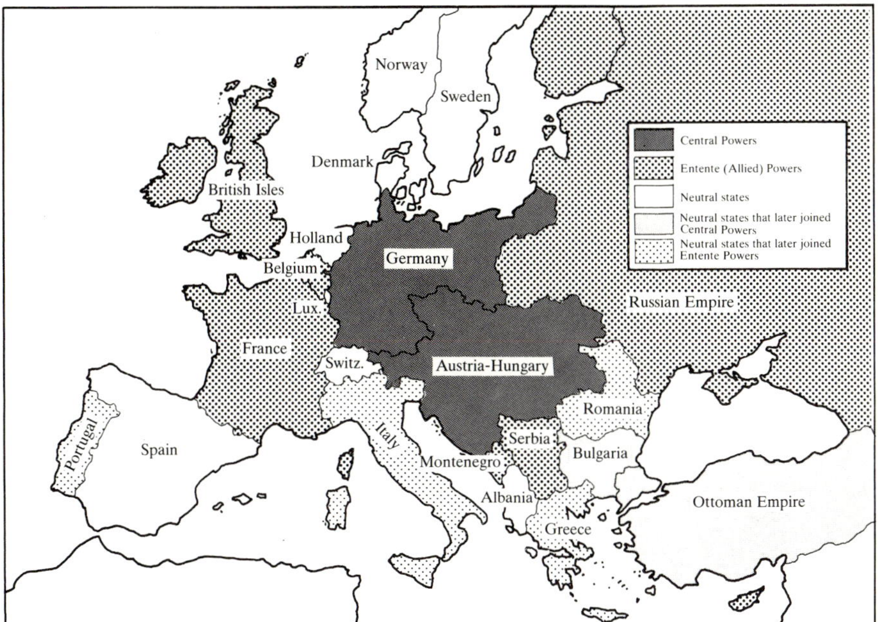

THE LINE-UP OF THE POWERS IN 1914

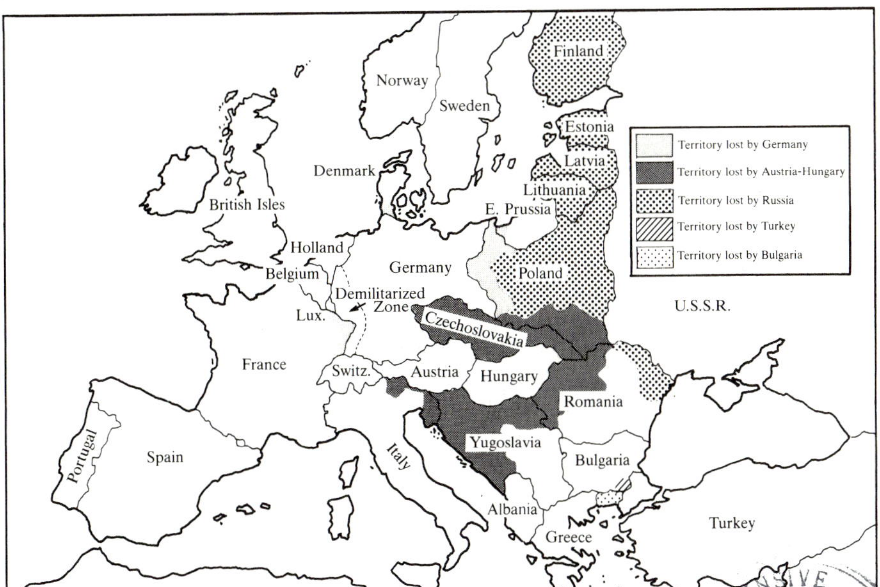

EUROPE 1919

The new states created by the Treaties of Brest-Litovsk and Versailles

reduced to 100,000 men, the navy to 15,000 and there was to be no air force at all. Finally, Germany was to pay a vast sum in reparations to compensate the Allies—this was to be paid off in instalments which were to continue until the 1980s.

As a final insult, the Germans had to accept sole responsibility for the war. Article 231 of the treaty—the War Guilt clause—stated: 'Germany accepts the responsibility of Germany and her allies for causing all the loss and damage to which the Allied and Associated Governments and their nationals have been subjected as a consequence of the war imposed on them by the aggression of Germany and

The Belgians welcome the arrival of liberating British troops.

Victory celebrations in London in 1919.

her allies.' The Germans regarded the peace as a Diktat (a dictated peace), as they were not allowed to take any part in the Versailles Conference which compiled the treaty. This created great anger in Germany and helped to pave the way for the success of the Nazis in the 1930s.

As J. M. Keynes, a leading British economist, commented: 'The Treaty includes no provisions for the economic rehabilitation of Europe—nothing to make the defeated Central Empires into good neighbours, nothing to stabilize the new States of Europe, nothing to reclaim Russia . . .'

The New States and their problems

Under the terms of the Treaty of St Germain (10th September 1919), the Austrian Empire was reduced to a small state centred on Vienna. By the Treaty of Trianon (4th June 1920), Hungary lost Croatia and

Architects of peace—left to right, Prime Minister Clemenceau of France, President Woodrow Wilson of the United States and Prime Minister Lloyd George of Great Britain.

Slovenia to Serbia and Montenegro: these areas formed the new state of Yugoslavia. Slovakia was taken from Hungary and united with the ex-Austrian lands of Bohemia and Moravia to make Czechoslovakia. Bulgaria ceded Thrace to Greece by the Treaty of Neuilly (27th November 1918). Large grants of Turkish lands were made to Greece under the Treaty of Sèvres (10th August 1920), but when the Greeks tried to take possession of these areas, they were defeated and driven out by the Turks led by Mustafa Kemal. The Great Powers had to accept the situation and legalize it by the Treaty of Lausanne (24th July 1923).

A number of new states appeared after the collapse of the Russian Empire. Poland obtained her independence and also received considerable territories from Germany and Austria—this created great resentment in Germany in particular and played some part in bringing about the Second World War. The Baltic States also received their freedom as the independent countries of Latvia, Lithuania and Estonia.

Even the victors were deeply affected by the war. The USA emerged as by far the most powerful country in the world. Britain was seriously weakened by the vast sums of money she had spent. France had suffered grievously and her economic progress was deeply affected between 1918 and 1939. The Italians were totally dissatisfied with the gains they received, paving the way for Mussolini and the Fascists to seize power. The Japanese and Chinese were equally disappointed and settled their differences by the Sino-Japanese War (1936–45). The Arabs were also disappointed in many of their hopes as the French took over the supervision of Syria and the British established mandates over Mesopotamia and Palestine. They were deeply angered when the British allowed the Jews to set up 'a national home' in Palestine—this decision led to the rise of the state of Israel and its wars with the neighbouring Arab states.

The Peace Conference at Versailles, in 1919.

A meeting of the Council of the League of Nations.

The League of Nations

The map of Europe and the world had been transformed by the peace treaties. Many new states had come into being. They needed time to settle down and overcome their economic, social and political problems. Most contained angry minorities who believed they were being discriminated against. The defences of the new states were weak and it was difficult to see how they could stand up to larger powers. President Wilson of the USA hoped that war and international disputes could be prevented by the creation of the League of Nations. Article 10 of the League's constitution reads: 'The members of the League undertake to respect and preserve as against external aggression the territorial integrity and existing political independence of all Members of the League.'

Unfortunately, the League was weakened by the USA's refusal to join. Although it brought economic, medical and educational aid to millions of people, it failed to control the aggressive actions of the Great Powers. The outbreak of the Second World War in 1939 demonstrated its weakness.

All this seems to show that the First World War settled nothing and that millions of people died in vain. But this is not the case. The new states that came into being after 1918 gradually developed into true nations. Although the League itself failed, its ideals were deeply respected and the world is still trying to realize them through the United Nations Organization. Although the nations of the world remain divided, people everywhere are trying to discover the secret of peaceful coexistence.

The price of war.

Table of War Fronts

Date	Western Front	Eastern Front
1914	*Aug 4* Germans enter Belgium British declare war *Sept 6–10* Battle of the Marne—German defeat	*Aug 7* Russians invade Prussia *Aug 26–9* Battle of Tannenberg—Russian defeat German invasion of Poland
1915	*Sept–Oct* Allied offensives in Artois and Champagne fail	*March* Russians invade Galicia *April* Austro-German counterattack *July* Russians withdraw from Galicia and Poland
1916	*Feb–Nov* Battle of Verdun—stalemate *July–Nov* Battle of Somme—stalemate	*June–Aug* Brusilov offensive Russians invade Galicia *Sept* Austro-German counter offensive
1917	*March* Germans retreat to Hindenburg Line *June* American troops arrive in France *July–Nov* Battle of Passchendaele—Allied defeat	*March* Bourgois Revolution *July* Last Russian Offensive defeated *Nov* Bolshevik Revolution
1918	*Mar* Last German offensive *Aug* Allied counterattack *Nov* Armistice	*Mar* Treaty of Brest-Litovsk *Aug* Allied landings at Archangel

Italian Front	Middle East	War at Sea
	Aug Turks driven behind Caucasus mountains	*Nov 1* Battle of Coronel—British defeat *Dec 8* Battle of Falkland Islands—British victory
May Italians declare war on Austria-Hungary First battle of the Isonzo	*April* Allied landings in Gallipoli *Dec* Allied evacuation of Gallipoli	*Feb* German submarine campaign opens *May* Lusitania sunk by German U-boat
Jan–Dec Series of battles along the Isonzo and Trentino	*April* British defeated at Kut in Mesopotamia *June* British advance into Southern Persia	*May/June* The battle of Jutland—indecisive
Last battle of the Isonzo *Oct* Battle of Caporetto—Austrian victory	*Feb* British recapture Kut *Dec* Jerusalem captured by Arabs and British	*Jan* Germans launch unrestricted submarine campaign *April* America declares war on Germany
June Austro-German offensive *Nov* Italian victory of Vittorio Veneto Armistice	*Sept* British take Damascus *Oct* Armistice	*Nov* German sailors mutiny at Kiel Armistice

GLOSSARY

Abdicate To renounce the throne.

Alliance The joining together of two or more countries by treaty for military purposes.

Annex To add territory by conquest or occupation.

Armistice A truce while the terms of a peace treaty are being worked out.

ASDIC Apparatus used for locating submarines by bouncing radio waves off the sea bed, developed by the Allied Submarine Detection Investigation Committee.

Balance of power The creation and maintenance of a state of equilibrium between powers; not allowing any one country to become too powerful.

Balkans A large peninsula in south-east Europe projecting into the Mediterranean Sea, including the modern states of Romania, Bulgaria, Greece, Yugoslavia and Albania.

Blockade The isolation of a state or states; and the prevention of the passage of goods or people into or out of a country.

Bolshevik Russian Social Democratic party.

Casualties People killed or wounded in war.

Central powers The First World War alliance of Germany, Austria, Turkey and Bulgaria.

Chief of the general staff A military commander responsible for the planning of an entire war on all fronts.

Coalition A group of powers uniting for a particular purpose.

Colony Overseas territory taken over and administered by a Great Power.

Commander-in-chief The military commander in charge of a particular front.

Conscientious objector A person with moral or religious objections to fighting.

Constitution The principles of government of a state.

Diktat A dictation—usually used with reference to the dictated Peace of Versailles.

Dreadnought A class of battleship introduced in 1905 which was entirely armed with big guns in turrets.

Economic imperialism The policy, dictated by economic needs, of extending a state's rule over other territories.

Entente A friendly understanding—used with reference to Britain's alliances with France and Russia as Britain made no military commitment.

Entente powers or **Allies** Russia, France and Britain.

Great Depression World-wide economic depression of the 1930s.

Incidents Confrontations between the Great Powers which carry the risk of war.

Mandate The authority given by the League of Nations to a Great Power to govern an underdeveloped country in the best interests of its inhabitants.

Marxist historians Those historians who believe that change is brought about by economic forces.

Mobilization Calling up the armed forces for active service.

Propaganda The organized promotion of particular views and beliefs to assist or damage the cause of a government or movement.

Reparation Sums paid by a conquered nation to the victors in compensation for war damage.

Shell shock A condition of serious nervous strain caused by prolonged engagement in warfare.

Socialists People who believe that the means of production, distribution and property should be nationalized; society should be classless; the national economy planned.

Suffragettes Militant women who demanded the right to vote in general elections, in the early years of the 20th century.

Sultan The ruler of the Turkish Empire until 1918.

Ultimatum A final demand under threat of war.

Zeppelin A large airship designed by Count Zeppelin (1838–1918).

FURTHER READING

Histories and accounts of the war

Cathcart Borer, M. *The First World War* (Signposts of History, Macmillan, 1970)

Evans, D. *The Great War 1914–18* (Links: Twentieth Century World History Books, Edward Arnold, 1981)

Gibbons, S. R. & Morican, P. *World War One* (Modern Times series, Longman, 1965)

Holden, Matthew *War in the Trenches* (Wayland, 1973)

Lloyd, A. *War in the Trenches* (Hart Davies, 1976)

Martin, Christopher *Battle of the Somme* (Wayland, 1983)

Parkinson, R. *The Origins of World War One* (Wayland, 1972)

Shermer, D. *World War I* (Octopus, 1972)

Taylor, A. J. P. *An Illustrated History of the First World War* (Hamish Hamilton, 1966)

Terraine, John *The Great War 1914–18* (Hutchinson, 1956)

Analyses of the war

Cruttwell, C. R. M. F. *A History of the Great War* (Oxford University Press, 1936)

Fall, C. *The Great War* (Putnam, 1959)

Liddell, B. H. *A History of the First World War* (Faber & Faber, 1936)

Marwick, A. *The Deluge* (Harmondsworth, Penguin, 1967)

Memoirs and documents

Graves, Robert *Goodbye to All That* (Penguin, 1960)

Kildoff, P. *The Red Baron* (Bailey Bros. & Swinfen, 1974)

Lawrence, T. E. *The Seven Pillars of Wisdom* (Cape, 1933)

Martin, Christopher *The War Poets* (Wayland, 1983)

Sassoon, Siegfried *The Memoirs of an Infantry Officer* (Faber & Faber, 1930)

PICTURE ACKNOWLEDGEMENTS

The illustrations in this book were supplied by: Mary Evans Picture Library 65; Imperial War Museum, London, *front cover*, 8, 13, 15, 18, 19, 20, 21, 22, 24, 25, 26, 27, 34, 38, 40, 42, 44, 46, 60, 64; Mansell Collection 6, 7, 10, 11, 12, 17, 23, 28, 29, 31, 32, 36, 39, 43, 48, 49, 62, 67, 69; Topham Picture Library 68. Maps on page 63 drawn by Malcolm S. Walker. The remaining pictures are from the Wayland Picture Library.

INDEX